SWEET TREATS FOR
CHRISTMAS

BY NANCY LAMBERT

PUBLISHING PLC

Published by Top That! Publishing plc
Tide Mill Way, Woodbridge, Suffolk, IP12 1AP, UK
www.topthatpublishing.com
Copyright © 2011 Top That! Publishing plc
All rights reserved.

CONTENTS

INTRODUCTION

Christmas is a special time of year, and the food that is prepared and enjoyed plays an important part. The magic and excitement can be even better if the food that is available not only tastes great, but is homemade as well.

Christmas is all about spending time with friends and family! A great way to have some festive fun is to get them involved in the cooking! Why not ask them to give you a hand with some of the recipes in this book?

This book will provide you with a selection of delicious festive recipes for adults and junior chefs to make together. And remember, once you have perfected the recipes, don't be afraid to experiment with the ingredients, fillings and toppings to create your own Christmas treats!

So, what are you waiting for? Get in the Christmas spirit and get cooking!

COOKING TIPS!

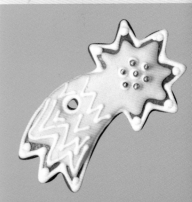

- Make sure you use the freshest ingredients possible.

- If you are making food for a specific day, prepare all you can in advance.

- Don't worry if you have made too much food – just keep it in the fridge or an airtight container for the next day, or freeze it for another time.

- Why not give away some of the little cookies or sweets as presents for your friends and family? Wrap them in brightly coloured festive paper!

EQUIPMENT

- To complete the recipes in this book, you will need to use a selection of everyday cooking equipment and utensils, such as mixing bowls, saucepans, a sieve, knives, spoons and forks and a chopping board.

- Of course, you'll need to weigh and measure the ingredients, so you'll need a measuring jug and some kitchen scales too.

- Some of the recipes tell you to use a whisk. Ask an adult to help you use an electric whisk, or you can use a balloon whisk yourself – you'll just have to work extra hard!

- To make some of the recipes in this book, you'll need to use the correct-sized tins or other special equipment. These items (and others that you may not have to hand) are listed at the start of each recipe.

SAFETY & HYGIENE

- Before starting any cooking always wash your hands.

- Cover any cuts with a plaster.

- Wear an apron to protect your clothes.

- Always make sure that all the equipment you use is clean.

- If you need to use a sharp knife to cut up something hard, ask an adult to help you. Always use a chopping board.

- Remember that trays in the oven and pans on the cooker can get very hot. Always ask an adult to turn on the oven and to get things in and out of the oven for you.

- Always ask an adult for help if you are using anything electrical – like an electric whisk.

- Be careful when heating anything in a pan on top of the cooker. Keep the handle turned to one side to avoid accidentally knocking the pan.

- Keep your pets out of the kitchen while cooking.

GETTING STARTED

MEASURING

Use scales to weigh exactly how much of each ingredient you need or use a measuring jug to measure liquids.

MIXING

Use a spoon, balloon whisk or electric hand whisk to mix the ingredients together.

DIFFERENT IDEAS

Decorate your festive treats with flavoured or coloured icing, and then add chocolate drops, sweets or sugar strands.

CREATING RECIPES

Once you've made a recipe in this book a few times, think about whether you could make your own version. Try to think up names for the things you create!

PLEASE NOTE

The measurements given in this book are approximate. Use the same measurement conversions throughout your recipe (grams or ounces) to maintain the correct ratios. All of the recipes in this book have been created for adults to make with junior chefs and must not be attempted by an unsupervised child.

Read through each recipe to make sure you've got all the ingredients that you need before you start.

CANDY CANES

Extra equipment:
- cling film
- rolling pin
- baking tray
- baking parchment
- spatula

Ingredients:
- 200 g (7 oz) butter
- 150 g (5 oz) caster sugar
- 2 teaspoons vanilla extract
- 1 egg
- 300 g (10 oz) plain flour, sifted
- red food colouring

1 Preheat the oven to 180°C / 350°F / gas mark 4.

2 Whisk the butter and sugar in a bowl, beat in the vanilla extract and the egg, and then add the flour. Beat until smooth, and then separate the mixture into two.

3 Blend one half of the mixture with red food colouring, adding drops until you get the depth of colour you want. Wrap both mixtures in cling film and place them in the refrigerator to chill for 30 minutes.

4 Roll both of the doughs out until they are 5 mm (1/4 in) thick. Ask an adult to cut the dough into 1/2 cm strips and chill for 5–10 minutes until slightly firm.

5 Take one of each colour, and press on top of the other. Twist the strips together to make a candy cane, pinching the ends. Repeat until all of the strips have been used.

6 Place onto a baking tray lined with baking parchment. Chill for 10 minutes, and then put them in the oven to bake for 8 minutes. Use a spatula to transfer the candy canes onto a wire rack to cool.

TOP TIP!
Decorate your tree with these canes or wrap and give as gifts!

HOT CHOCOLATE

Ingredients:

- 1 litre (1 ¾ pt) full cream milk
- 1 vanilla pod
- 150 g (5 oz) milk chocolate, broken into pieces
- whipped cream, to serve
- cocoa powder, to serve

1 Ask an adult to gently heat the milk with the vanilla pod.

2 Add the chocolate pieces.

3 Bring the mixture to the boil, stirring frequently, until the chocolate has melted.

4 Remove the vanilla pod and serve.

5 Serve with a squirt of whipped cream and a dusting of cocoa powder.

TOP TIP! For an extra treat, add a homemade candy cane!

11

CHRISTMAS PUDDING

Extra equipment:
- tea towel
- 1 litre (1 3/4 pt) pudding basin
- greaseproof paper
- foil
- string

Ingredients:
- 85 g (3 oz) mixed fruits
- 85 g (3 oz) dried cranberries
- 2 clementines, zest and juice
- 1 lemon, zest and juice
- 100 g (4 oz) softened butter
- 100 g (4 oz) dark muscovado sugar
- 50 g (2 oz) self-raising flour
- 1 teaspoon mixed spice
- 2 eggs, beaten
- 1 eating apple, peeled, cored, grated
- 50 g (2 oz) fresh white breadcrumbs
- 50 g (2 oz) glacé cherries, roughly chopped

1 Soak the mixed fruit, cranberries and zests in the clementine and lemon juices for 3 days, stirring daily, keeping the bowl covered with a tea towel.

2 Butter a 1 litre pudding basin and line the bottom with a greaseproof paper circle. Beat together the butter and sugar until pale and fluffy.

3 Sift in the flour and mixed spice, then stir in before adding the eggs.

4 Stir in the apple, soaked fruits and liquid and add the breadcrumbs and cherries, mixing thoroughly.

5 Fill the basin with the mixture, then cover with a double thickness of greaseproof paper, pleated in the middle. Cover this with a layer of foil, pleated in the middle, then tie tightly with string.

6 Place the pudding in a large saucepan on a trivet or upturned saucer so it doesn't touch the bottom, then ask an adult to fill halfway up the basin with hot water.

7 Bring to a simmer, cover the pan, and steam for 2 hours.

TOP TIP! Decorate your pudding with holly – don't eat the berries though!

CHRISTMAS TREE COOKIES

Extra equipment:
- baking tray
- cling film
- rolling pin
- festive cookie cutters
- clean plastic bag
- skewer
- several metres of fine ribbon or silver thread

Ingredients:
- 170 g (6 oz) plain flour
- 1/2 teaspoon ground mixed spice
- 50 g (2 oz) cocoa powder
- 100 g (4 oz) butter
- 100 g (4 oz) caster sugar
- 1 tablespoon milk
- 10 coloured boiled sweets

1 Preheat the oven to 180°C / 350°F / gas mark 4. Use a paper towel to grease the baking tray with a little butter.

2 Sift the flour, ground mixed spice and cocoa powder into a bowl. Cut the butter into cubes, add it to the flour, and rub the mixture through your fingertips until it looks crumbly.

3 Add the sugar and milk to the bowl, and knead the mixture into a soft dough. Wrap the dough in cling film and put it in the fridge for 15 minutes.

4 Put the dough onto a floured surface and roll it out. Use festive cookie cutters to cut out different shapes, and put them on the baking tray.

5 Put the boiled sweets in a plastic bag and crush them with a rolling pin. Carefully cut out a shape from the centre of each cookie. Fill the holes with the crushed sweets.

6 Use the skewer to pierce a hole in the top of each cookie.

7 Bake the cookies for 10–15 minutes, until they are cooked and the sweets have melted. Once the melted sweets have set, carefully lift the cookies onto a wire rack to cool.

8 Thread the hole at the top of each cookie with ribbon or thread, and hang them on your Christmas tree!

TOP TIP! You can also use a knife to cut your cookies into Christmassy shapes.

13

STAR TOPPED MINCE PIES

TOP TIP!
Why not top your mince pies with marzipan stars instead of pastry?

Extra equipment:

- rolling pin
- round pastry cutter
- star-shaped cookie cutter
- bun tin
- spatula

Ingredients:

- 200 g (8 oz) butter, softened
- 450 g (1 lb) plain flour
- 50 g (2 oz) icing sugar
- 2 egg yolks
- 3–4 tablespoons iced water
- 450 g (1 lb) mincemeat
- beaten egg, to glaze
- icing sugar, to decorate

1 Preheat the oven to 200°C / 400°F / gas mark 6.

2 Cut the butter into cubes. Sieve the flour into a mixing bowl. Add the butter and, using your fingertips, rub the butter into the flour until it resembles fine breadcrumbs.

3 Stir in the icing sugar. Make a well in the centre and stir in the egg yolks and about 3–4 tablespoons of iced water to make a soft but not sticky dough.

4 Knead lightly to form a smooth dough and chill for 30 minutes.

5 On a floured surface, roll out two thirds of the dough and cut out 30 rounds using the round pastry cutter. Use these to line the bun tin.

6 Fill the pie cases with mincemeat.

7 Re-roll the remaining pastry and trimmings and cut out stars using the star cookie cutter. Place onto the pies.

8 Brush the tops with beaten egg and cook for about 20 minutes or until they are golden brown. Use a spatula to transfer the mince pies to a wire rack to cool. Dust with icing sugar.

WINTER SNOW CUPCAKES

Extra equipment:
- bun tin
- paper cases
- piping bag

Ingredients:
- 125 g (4 1/2 oz) self-raising flour
- 125 g (4 1/2 oz) butter, softened
- 125 g (4 1/2 oz) caster sugar
- 2 large eggs
- 2–3 tablespoons milk
- 50 g (2 oz) white chocolate, broken into pieces

For the topping:
- whipped cream
- silver balls
- star sprinkles

1 Preheat the oven to 180°C / 350°F / gas mark 4. Place the bun cases in the bun tin.

2 Sift the flour into a bowl, then add the butter.

3 Use the tips of your fingers to rub the butter and flour together until the mixture becomes crumbly. Alternatively, ask an adult to use an electric whisk.

4 Add the sugar and mix it in, then stir in the eggs.

5 Finally, add the milk to make the mixture creamy, followed by the chocolate. Stir to mix.

6 Put spoonfuls of the mixture into the bun cases. Bake the cupcakes for 10–15 minutes, then leave them to cool on a wire rack.

7 Once cool, place the whipped cream in a piping bag and pipe onto the top of each cupcake. Finish by topping the cakes with silver balls and star sprinkles.

TOP TIP!
Look out for festive cupcake cases in supermarkets or craft shops!

BAKED RICE PUDDING

SERVES 4

Extra equipment:
- oven-proof pie dish

Ingredients:
- 550 ml (1 pt) milk
- 50 g (2 oz) pudding rice
- 25 g (1 oz) butter
- a few drops of vanilla essence
- 50 g (2 oz) sugar
- grated nutmeg

1 Preheat the oven to 150°C / 300°F / gas mark 2.

2 Ask an adult to boil the milk in a saucepan. Then, place the rice in a sieve, wash it well and then sprinkle it into the milk.

3 Add half of the butter, and the vanilla essence, and stir until the milk starts to boil again.

4 Simmer for 3–4 minutes and transfer into a buttered pie dish. Sprinkle with sugar, dot with the remaining pieces of butter and dust with freshly grated nutmeg.

5 Make sure that the edges of the dish are clean and transfer into a preheated oven. Cook until a rich brown skin forms on the top and the rice is cooked through (about 1–1 1/2 hrs).

TOP TIP!
Add a sprinkling of cinnamon to give this rice pudding a festive kick!

SANTA SNAPS

Extra equipment:
- baking tray
- greaseproof paper

Ingredients:
- 60 g (2 oz) butter
- 60 g (2 oz) caster sugar
- 60 g (2 oz) golden syrup
- 60 g (2 oz) flour
- 1/2 teaspoon ground ginger
- half a lemon

For the filling:
- 300 ml (1/2 pt) double cream
- 15 g (1/2 oz) icing sugar
- 240 g (8 1/2 oz) fresh fruit

1 Preheat the oven to 180°C / 350°F / gas mark 4.

2 Melt the butter, sugar and syrup in a small pan. Stir in the flour and ginger, add the grated rind of the half lemon and 1 tablespoon of the juice.

3 Place twelve tablespoons of the mixture well spaced on greaseproof paper and press them out. Bake them for 8–10 minutes until golden. Allow to cool slightly, and then slide off the paper onto a wire rack.

4 Whip the cream with the icing sugar until it forms soft peaks.

5 Spoon fresh cream into the middle of one snap, surround with fresh fruit and sandwich with a second snap. Repeat with a third, and decorate the top with cream and fruit.

6 Repeat the process to produce three more Santa Snaps.

TOP TIP!
Why not leave this out for Santa on Christmas Eve?

FESTIVE JAMMY DODGERS

TOP TIP!
Why not try using different-shaped cookie cutters?

Extra equipment:
- cling film
- rolling pin
- 2 star-shaped cookie cutters, one large and one small
- 2 baking trays

Ingredients:
- 225 g (8 oz) butter, softened
- 100 g (4 oz) caster sugar
- 200 g (7 oz) plain flour, plus extra for dusting
- 100 g (4 oz) ground almonds
- 100 g (4 oz) strawberry or raspberry jam

1 Preheat the oven to 140°C / 280°F / gas mark 1.

2 First, place the butter in a bowl and add the sugar. Beat together until light and fluffy and then add the flour and ground almonds. Mix well and then wrap in cling film. Leave in the fridge for at least an hour.

3 Remove the dough from the fridge and knead until it is soft enough to shape and roll. Sprinkle a little flour onto the work surface and then divide the dough into two balls. Using a rolling pin, roll out one of the balls of dough so it is about 5 mm (1/4 in) thick. Next, use the larger star cookie cutter to cut out stars. Place the stars on a baking tray. (These will be the bottom halves of the biscuits.)

4 Roll out the second ball of dough and repeat the same way. Once the second batch of stars are placed on a baking tray, use the smaller star-shaped cookie cutter to cut out the middle of each star, or use a knife. (These will be the top halves of the biscuits.)

5 Ask an adult to place the baking trays in the oven and cook for 20–30 minutes, until golden brown. Place on a wire rack to cool. Then, add a blob of jam to the centre of each of the bottom half biscuits (without the cut-out star). Finally, place the top halves of the biscuits onto the jam-covered ones and push down gently.

CHOCOLATE CAKE

Extra equipment:
- 20 cm (7 ¾ in) round cake tin
- greaseproof paper
- palette knife

Ingredients:
- 200 g (7 oz) dark chocolate
- 200 g (7 oz) butter, cut in pieces
- 1 tablespoon instant coffee granules
- 85 g (3 oz) self-raising flour
- 85 g (3 oz) plain flour
- ¼ teaspoon bicarbonate of soda
- 200 g (7 oz) light muscovado sugar
- 200 g (7 oz) golden caster sugar
- 25 g (1 oz) cocoa powder
- 3 eggs
- 75 ml (2 ½ fl.oz) buttermilk

For the topping:
- 200 g (7 oz) dark chocolate
- 284 ml (9 ½ fl.oz) carton double cream
- 2 tablespoons golden caster sugar

1 Preheat the oven to 160°C / 320°F / gas mark 3.

2 Butter the cake tin and line the base with greaseproof paper. Break the chocolate in pieces into a saucepan. Tip in the butter, then mix the coffee granules into 125 ml (4 fl.oz) of cold water and pour into the pan. Ask an adult to warm through over a low heat until everything has just melted.

3 While the chocolate is melting, mix the self-raising and plain flour, bicarbonate of soda, the two sugars and cocoa powder in a bowl, mixing with your hands to get rid of any lumps. Beat the eggs in a separate bowl and stir in the buttermilk.

4 Next, pour the melted chocolate mixture and the egg mixture into the flour mixture, stirring until everything is mixed to a smooth consistency. Pour this into the tin and bake for 1½ hours. Leave to cool in the tin, then turn out onto a wire rack to cool completely. Then, ask an adult to cut it into two.

5 To make the topping: ask an adult to chop the chocolate into small pieces and tip into a bowl. Pour the cream into a pan, add the sugar, and ask an adult to heat until it is about to boil. Take off the heat and pour it over the chocolate. Stir until the chocolate has melted and the mixture is smooth.

6 Sandwich the cake layers together with just a little of the topping. Pour the rest over the cake, smoothing to cover with a palette knife.

TOP TIP!
Insert a skewer into the cake. If it comes out clean, the cake is cooked!

CHRISTMAS CUPCAKES

TOP TIP! If you have any melted chocolate left over, dip marshmallows into it for a festive treat!

MAKES 10-12

Extra equipment:
- paper cases
- bun tin
- greaseproof paper
- Christmas decorations

Ingredients:
- 225 g (8 oz) self-raising flour
- 80 g (3 oz) butter, softened
- 80 g (3 oz) caster sugar
- 1 egg
- 80–100 ml (3–4 fl.oz) milk
- 100 g (4 oz) white chocolate
- sprinkles
- festive decoration (optional)

1 Preheat the oven to 180°C / 350°F / gas mark 4.

2 Sift the flour into a bowl, followed by the butter. Use the tips of your fingers to rub the butter and flour together until the mixture becomes crumbly.

3 Add the sugar and mix it in, then stir in the egg. Finally, add enough milk to make the mixture creamy.

4 Put spoonfuls of the mixture into the cupcake cases. Bake the cakes for 10–15 minutes, until they are golden brown, then leave them to cool on a rack.

5 While the cakes are cooling, put the white chocolate in a heatproof bowl. Ask an adult to put the bowl over a saucepan of simmering water (making sure the base doesn't touch the water). When the chocolate has melted, take the bowl off the pan.

6 Place the cooled cakes on a sheet of greaseproof paper and pour a little of the melted chocolate over the top. Before the chocolate sets, roll each cake in sprinkles and place a festive decoration on top to finish!

STOLLEN

Extra equipment:
- tea towel
- baking tray

Ingredients:
- 100 ml (3 ½ fl.oz) warm milk
- 2 teaspoons dried yeast
- pinch salt
- 225 g (8 oz) plain flour, plus extra for dusting
- 1 teaspoon caster sugar
- 1 teaspoon ground mixed spice
- 200 g (7 oz) mixed dried fruit
- 25 g (1 oz) flaked almonds
- 50 g (2 oz) unsalted butter
- 1 egg, beaten

To finish:
- 25 g (1 oz) butter, melted
- 50 g (2 oz) icing sugar

1 Place the milk and yeast into a bowl and mix well. Leave to rest for 5–6 minutes.

2 Meanwhile, sift the salt, flour, sugar and mixed spice into a large bowl. Add the dried fruit, almonds and butter and mix together.

3 Add the yeast and milk mixture, followed by the egg and mix together well to make a dough. Knead the dough for 5–6 minutes, and then cover with a tea towel and leave for 20 minutes.

4 Lightly dust the work surface with flour and place the dough onto it. Knead again for 3–4 minutes and then push and roll out by hand into an oval shape.

5 Place the stollen onto a greased baking tray and cover and place somewhere warm for one hour.

6 While the dough is rising, preheat the oven to 180°C / 350°F / gas mark 4.

7 Ask an adult to place the stollen in the oven for 40 minutes. Whilst still hot, brush the stollen with melted butter and dust with icing sugar.

8 Allow to cool and then serve in slices.

TOP TIP!
Traditional stollen includes marzipan! To add some to yours, roll 250 g (9 oz) into the centre of the stollen dough when shaping it in step 4, folding over the sides of the dough to seal in the marzipan!

DATE SQUARES

TOP TIP!
Substitute 30 g (1 oz) of flour for cocoa powder for a chocolatey twist!

MAKES 20

Extra equipment:
- food processor
- 20 x 28 cm (8 x 11 in) baking tin
- baking paper
- cling film

Ingredients:
- 400 g (14 oz) pitted dried dates
- 240 ml (8 fl.oz) water
- 1 teaspoon pure vanilla extract
- 200 g (7 oz) rolled oats
- 130 g (4 1/2 oz) plain flour
- 160 g (5 1/2 oz) light brown sugar
- 1/2 teaspoon baking soda
- 1/4 teaspoon salt
- 1/8 teaspoon ground cinnamon
- 225 g (8 oz) butter, cut into cubes

1 Preheat the oven to 180°C / 350°F / gas mark 4.

2 To make the date filling: Place the dates and water in a saucepan and ask an adult to cook them over a low heat, stirring occasionally, until the dates are soft and have absorbed most of the water (about 5–10 minutes). Remove from the heat and stir in the vanilla extract. Leave to cool and then place in the food processor and purée until smooth. Set aside.

3 Butter the baking tin and line the bottom with baking paper.

4 To make the oaty crust: Place the oats, flour, sugar, baking soda, salt and ground cinnamon into a bowl and mix well.

5 Then add the butter and combine until the mixture is crumbly. Press two thirds of the mixture into the base of the prepared baking tin.

6 Spread the date mixture evenly over the oaty crust and then sprinkle the remaining oat mixture evenly over the top of the dates. Bake for about 30–40 minutes or until golden brown. Place on a wire rack to cool.

7 Once it has cooled, cover the tin with cling film, and place in the refrigerator for at least one hour or until firm enough to cut easily into squares.

ALMOND BISCUITS

Extra equipment:
- rolling pin
- cookie cutters
- baking tray
- greaseproof paper
- pastry brush

Ingredients:
- 100 g (4 oz) butter, softened
- 50 g (2 oz) caster sugar
- 150 g (6 oz) self-raising flour
- 25 g (1 oz) ground almonds
- a few drops of almond extract
- 1 egg, beaten, to glaze

To decorate:
- 25 g (1 oz) whole almonds

1 Preheat the oven to 180°C / 350°F / gas mark 4.

2 Cream together the butter and sugar until light and fluffy.

3 Add the self-raising flour, ground almonds and almond extract and mix until you have a stiff dough mixture.

4 Roll out the dough to approximately 5 mm (1/4 in) thick. Cut out different festive shapes using cookie cutters or ask an adult to use a knife.

5 Place the biscuits onto a baking tray lined with a greaseproof paper. Glaze with beaten egg and finish your almond cookies by placing a whole almond on top.

6 Bake the biscuits for 10–15 minutes until golden brown.

7 Serve when cooled.

TOP TIP!
You can use cranberries or sweets as alternative toppings.

CHOCOLATE TRUFFLES

Extra equipment:
- plastic container
- sweet cases

Ingredients:
- 150 g (6 oz) plain chocolate
- 150 ml (5 fl.oz) double cream
- 25 g (1 oz) butter

To coat the truffles:
- cocoa powder
- chocolate strands
- chopped nuts

1 Ask an adult to put a heatproof bowl over a saucepan of just-simmering water, making sure the bowl doesn't touch the water. Break the plain chocolate into small pieces and put it into the bowl, and then add the cream and butter. Stir the mixture until the chocolate has melted.

2 Take the saucepan off the heat. Take the bowl off the saucepan and leave it to cool for a few minutes. Carefully pour the melted chocolate into a plastic container. Put the lid on the container and leave it in the fridge to set for 3–4 hours.

3 Remove the container from the fridge. Roll small balls of the chocolate truffle mixture in your hands.

4 Roll the balls in cocoa powder, chocolate strands or chopped nuts, and then put them into the sweet cases.

5 Store the truffles in a container in the fridge until you're ready to eat them or give them as a gift.

TOP TIP! Why not try using white chocolate as a yummy alternative?

COCONUT ICE

Extra equipment:
- 18 cm (7 in) square baking tin
- greaseproof paper

Ingredients:
- 225 g (8 oz) icing sugar
- 25 g (1 oz) butter
- 150 ml (5 fl.oz) sweetened condensed milk
- 225 g (8 oz) desiccated coconut, leaving some for decoration
- food colouring

1 Put the tin on the greaseproof paper, and draw around it. Cut out the square so that it is large enough to overlap the sides. Then, slit the corners and put it into the tin.

2 Ask an adult to help you put the icing sugar, butter and sweetened condensed milk into a pan over a medium heat, and bring the mixture to the boil. Let the mixture simmer for four minutes, stirring all the time.

3 Remove the pan from the heat and stir in the coconut.

4 Ask an adult to pour half of the mixture into the tin. Leave it to cool and set.

5 Colour the other half of the mixture with a few drops of food colouring. Pour it on top of the mixture in the tin, and leave it to set.

6 Cut the coconut ice into squares, but be careful – it will be very crumbly!

TOP TIP!
Once set, sprinkle the coconut ice with spare desiccated coconut!

25

CHOCOLATE OAT CRUNCHIES

Extra equipment:
- baking tray
- round cookie cutter

Ingredients:
- 100 g (4 oz) soft margarine
- 75 g (3 oz) demerara sugar
- 100 g (4 oz) plain wholemeal flour
- 100 g (4 oz) porridge oats
- 50 g (2 oz) chocolate chips

1 Preheat the oven to 180°C / 350°F / gas mark 4.

2 Use a paper towel to grease the baking tray with a little soft margarine.

3 Put the margarine and sugar into a bowl and mix them together with a wooden spoon.

4 Add the flour, oats and chocolate chips to the bowl. Mix everything together, using a spoon and then your hands, to make a soft dough.

5 Put the dough onto a floured surface and gently press it out.

6 Cut out circles of dough and put them onto the baking tray.

7 Bake the crunchies in the oven for 12–15 minutes, until they are golden brown. Place them onto a wire rack to cool.

TOP TIP! Try adding chopped nuts instead of chocolate chips for extra crunch!

ANGEL CAKES

Extra equipment:
- bun tin
- paper cases

Ingredients:
- 100 g (4 oz) butter
- 100 g (4 oz) caster sugar
- 2 eggs
- 100 g (4 oz) self-raising flour

For the topping:
- 80 g (3 oz) butter
- 150 g (5 oz) icing sugar
- 1–2 tablespoons milk
- icing sugar, to decorate

1 Preheat the oven to 180°C / 350°F / gas mark 4.

2 Put the butter and sugar into a mixing bowl. Use a wooden spoon to beat them together until the mixture is fluffy and very pale in colour. Beat in the eggs, one at a time, adding a tablespoon of flour with each one. Sift the rest of the flour into the bowl. Use a tablespoon to mix the ingredients gently. This will make sure your mixture stays nice and fluffy.

3 Use a teaspoon to transfer equal amounts of the mixture to the paper cases. Bake the buns for 20–25 minutes or until they are well risen and golden brown. Leave them to cool on a wire rack.

4 To make the butterfly wings, cut a slice from the top of each cake. Now cut each slice in half.

5 To make the buttercream topping, use a wooden spoon or an electric mixer to beat the butter in a large bowl until it is soft. Sift half of the icing sugar into the bowl, and then beat it with the butter until the mixture is smooth. Then, sift the rest of the icing sugar into the bowl and add one tablespoon of milk. Beat the mixture until it is smooth and creamy.

6 Place a little buttercream icing on top of each bun. Now, gently push two of the halved slices into the icing on each bun at an angle to form pretty butterfly wings. Dust with icing sugar to finish.

TOP TIP!
Make sure the buns are completely cold before cutting the angel wings!

MINCEMEAT PARCELS

Extra equipment:
- baking tray
- pastry brush

Ingredients:
- 4 sheets of ready-prepared filo pastry
- 60 g (2 oz) butter, melted
- 120 g (4 oz) mincemeat
- 1 egg yolk

1 Preheat the oven to 200°C / 400°F / gas mark 6.

2 Take one sheet of filo pastry and brush with a little melted butter. Fold in half to sandwich the butter, then cut the sheet into four equal quarters.

3 Carefully butter the top of one quarter. Place a second quarter on top at a slight angle, butter this and repeat the process with a third and fourth square – you should have a star shape.

4 Place a spoonful of mincemeat in the centre, brush round the mincemeat with egg yolk whisked with a little water.

5 Draw up the points of the star to form a purse and pinch the pastry together in the middle to stick. Arrange the pointed tips of the star in a decorative fashion.

6 Brush the parcels with melted butter and bake for 10–15 minutes or until golden and crisp.

7 Allow to cool slightly before serving. For a more festive look dust them with icing sugar.

TOP TIP! Serve with double cream or vanilla ice cream.

YULE LOG

Extra equipment:
- 30 x 40 cm (12 x 15 in) Swiss roll tin
- greaseproof paper

Ingredients:
- butter, for greasing
- 5 eggs
- 140 g (5 oz) caster sugar
- 100 g (3 1/2 oz) self-raising flour
- 35 g (1 1/2 oz) cocoa powder

For the icing:
- 150 g (5 oz) dark chocolate
- 80 g (3 oz) unsalted butter
- 300 g (10 1/2 oz) icing sugar, sieved
- 75 ml (2 3/4 fl.oz) whole milk

1 Preheat the oven to 180°C / 350°C / gas mark 4. Grease the tin with butter and line with greaseproof paper.

2 Ask an adult to bring a little water to simmering in a pan. Place a heatproof bowl over the water, making sure the base doesn't touch the water. Place the eggs and sugar in the bowl and whisk for 8–10 minutes, or until pale and fluffy.

3 Add the self-raising flour and cocoa powder and fold until well combined.

4 Spoon the mixture into the Swiss roll tin, then transfer to the oven and bake for 12–15 minutes, or until the cake springs back when pressed. Turn the cake out onto a sheet of greaseproof paper, then roll up and set aside for at least one hour to cool.

5 For the icing, place a heatproof bowl over the pan of simmering water, making sure the base of the bowl doesn't touch the water. Add the chocolate and butter and stir until melted, glossy and well combined. Add the icing sugar and beat together well, then stir in the milk and set aside to cool.

6 Unroll the cake and spread one third of the icing onto it in an even layer, then roll it up again.

7 Spread the remaining icing on top of the cake and dust with cocoa powder and icing sugar.

TOP TIP! Decorate your Yule Log with festive decorations to make a table centre piece!

SNOWBALLS

Extra equipment:
- electric whisk (optional)
- baking tray
- greaseproof paper
- pastry brush

Ingredients:
- 75 g (2 ½ oz) icing sugar
- 225 g (8 oz) butter, softened
- 2 teaspoons vanilla essence
- 250 g (9 oz) plain flour
- 90 g (3 oz) nuts, pecans or almonds finely chopped
- ½ teaspoon salt

To decorate:
- apricot jam
- desiccated coconut

1 Preheat the oven to 170°C / 325°F / gas mark 3.

2 With a wooden spoon or electric whisk, mix the icing sugar, butter and vanilla essence together in a mixing bowl until you have a smooth paste.

3 Add the flour, nuts and salt to the mixture and stir. Keep mixing until all the ingredients are combined and you have a smooth dough.

4 Using a teaspoon, spoon balls of the dough onto a baking tray lined with greaseproof paper.

5 Bake the snowballs for 15–20 minutes. They should be just golden, so make sure you don't overcook them!

6 Ask an adult to remove the hot tray from the oven. While the snowballs are still warm, brush with a little apricot jam and then roll them across a plate of desiccated coconut.

7 Leave the decorated cookies on a wire rack to cool.

TOP TIP!
Serve the snowballs in paper cases and give them away as little gifts!

STRAWBERRY SHORTBREAD TREES

Extra equipment:
- rolling pin
- tree-shaped cookie cutters
- baking tray

Ingredients:
- 130 g (4 1/2 oz) butter, softened
- 60 g (2 1/2 oz) caster sugar
- 130 g (4 1/2 oz) plain flour
- 60 g (2 1/2 oz) rice flour
- pinch salt
- 50 g (2 oz) strawberry jam

1 Preheat the oven to 170°C / 325°F / gas mark 3.

2 Cream the butter and sugar together in a large bowl, until pale and fluffy. Add both flours and the salt and mix well.

3 Use your hands to bring the mixture together and then place it on a floured work surface. Using a rolling pin, roll out the dough so it is about 5 mm (1/4 in) thick.

4 Next, use a tree-shaped cookie cutter to cut out trees (or ask an adult to cut the shapes using a knife). Roll out the leftover trimmings and keep cutting out trees. Place the trees on a greased baking tray.

5 Bake for 30–35 minutes, or until pale golden brown. Place on a wire rack to cool.

6 Then, add a blob of jam to half of the trees and spread. Place the other halves of the biscuits onto the jam-covered ones and push down gently. Finally, add blobs of jam to the top of the biscuits!

TOP TIP!
Try making different-coloured trees by using different-flavoured jams!

SNOWFLAKE SQUARES

Extra equipment:

• 22 x 33 cm (9 x 13 in) baking tin
• greaseproof paper
• forks, to serve

Ingredients:

• 50 g (2 oz) butter
• 1 teaspoon vanilla extract
• 200 g (7 oz) marshmallows
• 100 g (4 oz) crisped rice cereal

1 Wipe around the sides and bottom of the baking tin with a little oil or butter on a paper towel.

2 In a large saucepan, ask an adult to melt the butter over a low heat. Add the vanilla extract and melt the marshmallows into the butter, stirring.

3 Add the rice cereal when the marshmallows have melted and stir until the cereal is coated. Quickly pour into the tin. Use a sheet of greaseproof paper to press the mixture down flat and evenly into the tin.

4 Let the snowflakes set for 2 to 3 hours. Cut into squares and insert forks into them for easy eating!

TOP TIP!
Why not add sweets or chocolate buttons along with the crisped cereal?

32

CHRISTMAS ICED CUPCAKES

Extra equipment:
- bun tray
- bun cases
- rolling pin
- cookie cutters, various shapes

Ingredients:
- 100 g (4 oz) self-raising flour
- 1 tablespoon cocoa powder
- 125 g (4 1/2 oz) butter, softened
- 125 g (4 1/2 oz) caster sugar
- 2 large eggs
- 2–3 tablespoons milk

For the topping:
- ready-to-roll icing
- red food colouring
- green food colouring
- sweets or silver balls

1 Preheat the oven to 180°C / 350°F / gas mark 4.

2 Sift the flour and cocoa powder into a bowl, followed by the butter. Use the tips of your fingers to rub the butter, flour and cocoa powder together until the mixture becomes crumbly.

3 Add the sugar and mix it in, then stir in the eggs.

4 Finally, add the milk to make the mixture creamy.

5 Put spoonfuls of the mixture into the bun cases. Bake the cupcakes for 10–15 minutes, then leave them to cool on a wire rack.

6 For the topping, roll out some of the ready-to-roll icing and cut out shapes with cookie cutters. Lay over a few of the cupcakes.

7 Next, knead a couple of drops of red food colouring into some of the remaining icing. When the colour is even, roll out the icing and cut out festive shapes. Repeat the process, this time with the green food colouring.

8 Lay the different shapes over the tops of the rest of the cupcakes and finish with sweets or silver balls.

TOP TIP!
Pipe extra decorations onto the top of the cupcakes with royal icing, using a piping bag with a thin nozzle.

FRUIT AND NUT LOAF

Extra equipment:

- clean cloth
- 22 cm x 10 cm (9 in x 5 in) loaf tin

Ingredients:

- 75 g (2 3/4 oz) sultanas
- 75 g (2 3/4 oz) glacé cherries
- 300 ml (1/2 pint) tepid Earl Grey tea
- 250 g (9 oz) self-raising flour
- 200 g (7 oz) soft light brown sugar
- 75 g (2 3/4 oz) walnuts and pecans
- 1 egg, beaten
- 1 teaspoon ground cinnamon
- 1 teaspoon freshly grated nutmeg
- butter, for greasing

1 Place the sultanas, cherries and tea into a large bowl. Cover the bowl with a clean cloth and leave to soak overnight.

2 The next day, preheat the oven to 175°C / 325°F / gas mark 3.

3 Add the flour, sugar, nuts, beaten egg and spices to the soaked fruit and mix well.

4 Grease the loaf tin and pour in the mixture.

5 Transfer to the oven and bake for 1 1/4 hours, or until a skewer inserted into the cake comes out clean.

6 Leave the cake to cool for 10 minutes and then turn out of the tin and place on a wire rack to cool completely. Cut into slices to serve.

TOP TIP!
Experiment with different dried fruits – try adding raisins, currants or even dried apricots!

HOT SPICED APPLE

Ingredients:
- 3 litres (6 1/4 pints) cloudy apple juice
- 100 g (3 1/2 oz) brown sugar
- 1 teaspoon whole cloves
- 1 teaspoon whole allspice
- 3 cinnamon sticks
- grated rind of 1 orange
- star anise (optional)

1 Pour the apple juice into a large saucepan and stir in the brown sugar.

2 Add the cloves, allspice, cinnamon sticks and orange rind.

3 Bring the apple juice to a boil, stirring regularly. Once boiling, lower the temperature to a simmer. Simmer for about 15 minutes to allow the spices to infuse, stirring occasionally.

4 Then, take the juice off the heat and strain to remove the large spices.

5 Pour into glasses and decorate with a couple of cinnamon sticks and a star anise (optional). Serve immediately.

TOP TIP! Choose pretty glasses to serve your spiced apple in to add a festive feel.

35

GINGERBREAD COOKIES

TOP TIP!
For extra sparkle press edible silver balls onto the icing!

MAKES 30

Extra equipment:
• cling film • greaseproof paper
• rolling pin • cookie cutters
• baking tray • piping bag
• ribbon

Ingredients:
• 75 g (2 1/2 oz) soft brown sugar
• 2 tablespoons golden syrup
• 1 tablespoon black treacle
• 1 teaspoon cinnamon
• 1 teaspoon ginger
• 1 teaspoon ground cloves
• 100 g (3 1/2 oz) butter, softened
• 1/2 teaspoon bicarbonate of soda
• 225 g (8 oz) plain flour

To decorate:
• 50 g (2 oz) icing sugar
• 1 tablespoon orange juice
• food colouring (optional)

1 Preheat the oven to 180°C / 350°F / gas mark 4.

2 Put the sugar, syrup, treacle, cinnamon, ginger, ground cloves and a tiny bit of water into a pan. Ask an adult to heat up the mixture, stirring all the time with a wooden spoon, until it is bubbling.

3 Take the pan off the heat, then stir in the butter, bicarbonate of soda and flour until you have a smooth dough. Wrap the dough in a piece of cling film and place in the fridge for 30 minutes.

4 Place the dough onto a sheet of greaseproof paper, then put another sheet on top.

5 Using a rolling pin, roll the dough flat between the sheets until it is 3 mm (1/8 in) thick.

6 Using cookie cutters or a sharp knife, cut out cookies from the dough. Pierce a hole in the top of each cookie.

7 Place the cookies onto a baking tray covered with a sheet of greaseproof paper and bake for 15–20 minutes, until they are firm. Transfer the cookies to a wire rack to cool.

8 To decorate, mix the icing sugar and orange juice and add a few drops of food colouring if you want. Spread icing on the cookies, piping on finer details. Use ribbon to hang the cookies as decorations.

36

BREAD AND BUTTER PUDDING

Extra equipment:
- oven-proof pie dish
- electric whisk (optional)

Ingredients:
- 8 slices white bread
- 50 g (2 oz) butter
- 50 g (2 oz) sultanas
- 25 g (1 oz) caster sugar
- 25 g (1 oz) apricot jam

For the custard:
- 3 large egg yolks
- 2 tablespoons golden caster sugar
- a few drops of vanilla essence
- 300 ml (10 fl.oz) milk

1 Preheat the oven to 180°C / 350°F / gas mark 4.

2 First, make the custard by whisking the eggs, sugar and vanilla essence together. Then, slowly add the milk, whisking all the time.

3 Cut the crusts off the bread and lightly butter each slice. Next, lay in a buttered pie dish in a neat overlapping pattern, and sprinkle with sultanas.

4 Partly cover the bread slices with some of the custard.

5 Leave to stand to allow the custard to soak in. Then, add the rest of the mixture and sprinkle with the caster sugar.

6 Wipe the edges of the dish and bake in a preheated oven for approximately 45 minutes to 1 hour or until the custard is set and the bread is golden and crispy.

7 When the pudding has cooled slightly, brush with a little apricot jam. Serve warm!

TOP TIP!
Try adding chocolate chips instead of sultanas for a chocolatey treat!

SNOWBALL CAKE POPS

Extra equipment:
- 8 lollipop sticks
- baking tray
- greaseproof paper

Ingredients:
- 100 g (3 ½ oz) dark chocolate
- 125 g (4 ½ oz) fruit cake
- 125 g (4 ½ oz) Madeira cake
- 2 tablespoons desiccated coconut
- 2 tablespoons chopped hazelnuts

To decorate:
- 300 g (10 ½ oz) white chocolate

1 Ask an adult to melt the dark chocolate in a bowl set over a pan of simmering water, making sure the base of the bowl doesn't touch the water.

2 Crumble the fruit cake and Madeira cake into a bowl, then stir in the melted chocolate, desiccated coconut and hazelnuts until well combined.

3 Roll golf ball sized pieces of the mixture into balls. Stick a wooden stick into each ball and set aside in the fridge for 20–30 minutes, or until firm.

4 Then, ask an adult to melt the white chocolate in a bowl set over a pan of simmering water, making sure the base of the bowl doesn't touch the water.

5 Line the baking tray with greaseproof paper.

6 Remove the balls from the fridge. Dip each in the melted chocolate, making sure they are all completely coated.

7 Place onto the baking tray and set aside in the refrigerator for 20–30 minutes, or until the chocolate has set.

TOP TIP!
This recipe works just as well with a dark or milk chocolate coating!

38

SNOWFLAKE CUPCAKES

Extra equipment:
- bun tray
- bun cases
- rolling pin

Ingredients:
- 3 eggs
- 150 g (5 oz) butter, softened
- 150 g (5 oz) sugar
- 175 g (6 oz) self-raising flour, sifted
- a few drops of vanilla essence

For the topping:
- blue food colouring
- ready-to-roll icing
- edible glitter, to decorate

1 Preheat the oven to 180°C / 350°F / gas mark 4.

2 Crack the eggs into a bowl and beat lightly with a fork. Add the beaten eggs to a large bowl containing the butter, sugar, sifted flour and vanilla essence.

3 Beat until the mixture is light and creamy.

4 Use a teaspoon to transfer equal amounts of the mixture to the bun cases. Bake the cupcakes for 18–20 minutes. Leave them to cool on a wire rack.

5 Knead a couple of drops of food colouring into half of the ready-to-roll icing. When the colour is even, roll out the icing and cut out blue snowflake shapes to cover each cupcake.

6 Cut out smaller snowflake shapes from the remaining ready-to-roll icing and place these on top of the blue icing base layer. Sprinkle with edible glitter to finish.

TOP TIP!
You could use marzipan instead of icing for the topping!

CINNAMON DOUGHNUTS

MAKES 14-16

Extra equipment:
• rolling pin

Ingredients:
• 2 eggs
• 100 g (3 ½ oz) caster sugar
• 1 vanilla pod, seeds scraped out
• 100 ml (3 ½ fl.oz) crème fraîche
• 375 g (13 ½ oz) plain flour, plus extra for dusting
• pinch salt
• 1 tablespoon baking powder
• 1 teaspoon bicarbonate of soda
• vegetable oil, for deep frying
• 2 teaspoons cinnamon, to decorate
• 3 tablespoons caster sugar, to decorate

1 In a bowl, beat the eggs, sugar and vanilla seeds for five minutes, then stir in the crème fraîche.

2 Sift in the flour, salt, baking powder and bicarbonate of soda and mix well. Knead on a floured surface for 2–3 minutes until a smooth dough forms.

3 Roll out the dough to about 5 mm (½ in) thick and cut out 7.5 cm (3 in) circles. Make a small hole in the centre of each doughnut.

4 Ask an adult to half-fill a large saucepan with vegetable oil and heat until a small cube of bread turns golden in 30 seconds. **Do not leave hot oil unattended.**

5 Ask an adult to fry the doughnuts in the oil for 3–4 minutes, or until golden brown. Do this in batches to avoid over-crowding the pan.

6 In a small bowl mix the cinnamon and caster sugar.

7 Once the doughnuts have cooled slightly, roll each in the sugar mix until well covered.

TOP TIP! For filled doughnuts, shape into circles and fry. Once cooked, pipe in custard or jam!

40

WHITE FESTIVE FUDGE

Extra equipment:

- 15 cm (6 in) square baking tin
- greaseproof paper
- ribbon (optional)

Ingredients:

- 300 g (10 oz) white chocolate
- 2 teaspoons vanilla essence
- 200 ml (7 fl.oz) sweetened condensed milk
- 90 g (3 oz) dried cranberries, chopped

1 Line the tin with greaseproof paper.

2 Ask an adult to help you put the chocolate, vanilla essence and condensed milk into a saucepan over a medium heat. Stir them together until the chocolate has melted.

3 Take off the heat and add the chopped dried cranberries. Mix well.

4 Ask an adult to pour the mixture into the tin, and smooth the top with the back of a metal spoon. When cooled, put the tin into the fridge for 3–4 hours.

5 Remove the fudge from the tin by lifting it with the greaseproof paper. Turn it out onto a board and peel off the paper.

6 Cut the slab of fudge into squares and serve!

TOP TIP!
Tie with ribbons or put into paper cases for pretty gifts!

FRUITY CRUMBLE

Extra equipment:
- 23 cm (9 in) ovenproof dish

Ingredients:
- 30 g (1 ½ oz) unsalted butter
- 3 large cooking apples, peeled, cored and sliced
- 150 g (5 ½ oz) caster sugar
- 80 g (3 oz) blackberries

For the crumble topping:
- 110 g (4 oz) plain flour
- 50 g (1 ½ oz) unsalted butter, diced
- 55 g (2 oz) caster sugar

1 Preheat the oven to 180°C / 350°F / gas mark 4.

2 For the crumble filling, heat the butter in a pan over a medium heat. Add the apple slices and fry for 3–4 minutes, or until softened.

3 Add the sugar and stir well to coat the apples. Continue to cook until the apples are tender and golden brown and the sugar has melted.

4 Add the blackberries and stir gently to combine.

5 For the crumble topping, sift the flour into a large mixing bowl. Add the butter and sugar and rub together, using your fingertips, until the mixture resembles breadcrumbs.

6 Spoon the apple and blackberry filling into the ovenproof dish. Sprinkle over the topping mixture to just cover the filling.

7 Place into the oven and bake for 20 minutes, or until the topping is pale golden brown and the filling is bubbling.

TOP TIP! Serve hot with custard or ice cream for a winter treat!

ICED SHORTBREAD SNOWFLAKES

Extra equipment:
- greaseproof paper
- snowflake cookie cutter or a sharp knife
- rolling pin
- baking tray
- spatula
- piping bag

Ingredients:
- 100 g (3 1/2 oz) butter, softened
- 60 g (2 oz) golden caster sugar
- 100 g (3 1/2 oz) plain flour
- 60 g (2 oz) fine semolina

To decorate:
- 50 g (2 oz) icing sugar
- 1 tablespoon orange juice
- food colouring (optional)
- silver balls

1 Preheat the oven to 150°C / 300°F / gas mark 2.

2 Put the butter and sugar into a mixing bowl. Using a wooden spoon, mix them together until they make a smooth paste. Sift the flour into the bowl. Add the semolina and then stir the mixture well.

3 Then, use your hands to knead the mixture. The dough will be ready when it is smooth and there are no bits left on the sides of the bowl.

4 Place the mixture on top of a sheet of greaseproof paper, then put another sheet on top. Using a rolling pin, roll the dough flat between the sheets until it is about 3 mm (1/8 in) thick.

5 Use a snowflake-shaped cookie cutter or a sharp knife to cut out shapes from the dough. Lay the shapes on a baking tray lined with greaseproof paper.

6 Bake the shortbread for 15–20 minutes. Ask an adult to remove the hot tray from the oven. Use a spatula to lift the snowflakes onto a wire rack to cool.

7 To decorate, mix together the icing sugar and orange juice and mix to form a paste. Add a few drops of food colouring if you want.

8 Spread the icing over the shortbread, piping on finer details. Finish with sparkly silver balls.

TOP TIP! Experiment with different coloured icings to jazz up these shortbread cookies.

COCONUT MACAROONS

Extra equipment:
- baking tray
- greaseproof paper

Ingredients:
- 2 egg whites
- 1/4 teaspoon cream of tartar
- 100 g (4 oz) caster sugar
- 30 g (1 oz) ground almonds
- pinch of salt
- 1 teaspoon vanilla extract
- 250 g (9 oz) shredded coconut

1 Preheat the oven to 170°C / 340°F / gas mark 3. Line the baking tray with greaseproof paper.

2 Whisk the egg whites in a mixing bowl until frothy, add the cream of tartar and continue beating until they form soft peaks.

3 Add the sugar a teaspoon at a time, whisking until the peaks hold their shape.

4 Mix in the almonds, salt, vanilla and coconut.

5 Using a tablespoon, place dollops of the mixture, about 6 cm (2 1/2 in) wide, onto the baking tray. Leave enough space between each macaroon to expand during cooking.

6 Cook the macaroons for 20 minutes, or until they are turning golden brown. Remove from the oven and cool on a wire rack.

TOP TIP!
Try adding 1/2 teaspoon of lemon or lime juice for a zingy flavour.

PARTY CAKES

Extra equipment:
- bun tray
- paper cases
- piping bag

Ingredients:
- 125 g (4 1/2 oz) self-raising flour
- 125 g (4 1/2 oz) butter, softened
- 125 g (4 1/2 oz) caster sugar
- 2 large eggs
- a few drops of vanilla extract
- 2–3 tablespoons milk

For the topping:
- whipped cream
- sugar sprinkles

1 Preheat the oven to 180°C / 350°F / gas mark 4.

2 Sift the flour into a bowl, followed by the butter. Use the tips of your fingers to rub the butter and flour together until the mixture becomes crumbly. Alternatively, ask an adult to use an electric whisk.

3 Add the sugar and mix it in, then stir in the eggs. Finally, add the vanilla extract and milk to make the mixture creamy.

4 Put spoonfuls of the mixture into the bun cases. Bake the cupcakes for 10–15 minutes, until they are golden brown, then leave them to cool on a wire rack.

5 Once cool, place the whipped cream into a piping bag and pipe onto the top of the cupcakes.

6 Finish with sugar sprinkles.

TOP TIP! For a bit of Christmas sparkle, try adding edible glitter as an alternative decoration!

45

JELLY DELIGHT

Extra equipment:
• small square dish

Ingredients:
• 135 g (5 oz) strawberry, raspberry or orange jelly

To decorate:
• icing sugar

1 Cut the jelly into cubes and put it into a heatproof jug. Ask an adult to prepare the jelly, following the packet instructions.

2 Stir the jelly with a wooden spoon until it has dissolved. Pour the jelly into the dish and put it in the fridge to set.

3 When the jelly has set, loosen the edges from the dish and cut it into squares.

4 Carefully turn the jelly out onto a plate or board covered in icing sugar. Turn the squares of jelly until they are completely covered.

TOP TIP!
Try coating the jelly delights in melted chocolate then rolling in coconut or nuts for an alternative sweet treat!

ORANGE AND CRANBERRY MUFFINS

Extra equipment:
- muffin tray
- paper cases

Ingredients:
- 250 g (9 oz) plain flour
- 150 g (5 oz) sugar
- 1 tablespoon baking powder
- 1 egg
- 175 ml (6 fl.oz) milk
- 3 tablespoons vegetable oil
- 80 g (1 oz) chopped cranberries
- 2 tablespoons grated orange peel
- 2 tablespoons chopped pecans
  or walnuts

1 Preheat the oven to 190°C / 375°F / gas mark 5.

2 Put the paper cases in the muffin tray.

3 Sift the flour, sugar and baking powder into a bowl, and mix them together.

4 Pour in the egg, milk and vegetable oil and mix until all the flour is combined.

5 Fold in the cranberries, orange peel and nuts until distributed evenly throughout the mixture.

6 Use a teaspoon to transfer equal amounts of the mixture to the paper cases. Bake the muffins for 20 minutes or until they are well risen and golden brown.

7 Leave them to cool on a wire rack.

TOP TIP!
Substitute the cranberries for blueberries for a classic muffin taste.

CHRISTMAS CAKE

Extra equipment:
- 18 cm (7 in) round cake tin
- palette knife
- wide decorative ribbon (optional)

Ingredients:
- 100 g (4 oz) margarine
- 1 large egg
- 1 tablespoon pear and apple spread or thick honey
- 150 g (6 oz) self-raising wholemeal flour
- 225 g (8 oz) mincemeat
- orange juice

To decorate:
- 100 g (4 oz) icing sugar
- 1-2 tablespoons orange juice

1 Preheat the oven to 160°C / 325°F / gas mark 3.

2 Grease the cake tin with a little margarine.

3 Put the margarine, egg and pear and apple spread (or honey) in a bowl and mix them together until they're light and creamy.

4 Sift the flour into the bowl, and mix it in gently. Add the mincemeat and mix well. Then add enough orange juice to make a soft mixture.

5 Put the mixture into the tin, smoothing the top with the spoon. Bake for 40 minutes, until it is golden brown.

6 Leave the cake in the tin for five minutes, and then turn it out onto a wire rack to cool.

7 Sieve the icing sugar into a bowl, and mix in enough orange juice to make a thick paste. Spoon the mixture over the cake, covering the top and sides and smoothing with a palette knife. Leave to set.

TOP TIP!
Tie a wide ribbon around your cake and add festive decorations.

48

CHOCOLATE FUDGE BROWNIES

Extra equipment:
- 20 cm (8 in) square cake tin
- baking parchment

Ingredients:
- 2 eggs
- 225 g (8 oz) caster sugar
- 100 g (4 oz) butter
- 3 tablespoons cocoa powder
- 100 g (4 oz) self-raising flour
- 50 g (2 oz) pecans, chopped

For the topping:
- 50 g (2 oz) butter
- 1 tablespoon milk
- 100 g (4 oz) icing sugar
- 2 tablespoons cocoa powder
- pecan or walnut halves,
  to decorate

1 Preheat the oven to 180°C / 350°F / gas mark 4.

2 Beat the eggs and the sugar together in a bowl, until light and fluffy.

3 Ask an adult to melt the butter in the microwave (5 seconds max) and beat in the cocoa powder before adding to the eggs and sugar.

4 Sift the self-raising flour and fold into the main mixture with the chopped pecans.

5 Grease a 20 cm (8 in) square cake tin with butter, then line it with baking parchment. Pour in the mixture and bake in the oven for 40–45 minutes.

6 For the topping, melt the butter in a small pan and add the milk. Remove from the heat, then beat in the icing sugar and cocoa powder.

7 Spread icing over the cooked brownies and decorate with pecans or walnut halves. Cut into squares when the topping is firm.

TOP TIP!
If you don't like nuts, try mixing in some chocolate chips or raisins!

WHITE CHOCOLATE DROPS

MAKES 8-10

Extra equipment:
- baking tray
- greaseproof paper

Ingredients:
- 170 g (6 oz) white chocolate
- a handful each of:
  dried apricots, chopped
  pistachios
  raisins
  candied fruits, chopped
  walnuts, chopped

1 Line a baking tray with greaseproof paper.

2 Place a heatproof bowl over a pan of simmering water, making sure the bottom doesn't touch the water. Add the white chocolate in chunks.

3 Stir the chocolate, until melted.

4 Use a tablespoon to pour spoonfuls of the melted chocolate onto the greaseproof paper to form discs.

5 Sprinkle each with the fruit and nuts and place in the refrigerator to set.

6 Once set, peel each disc off the greaseproof paper and enjoy!

TOP TIP!
Try using milk or dark chocolate, or experiment with different toppings.

TOFFEE PUDDING

Extra equipment:

- medium heatproof pudding basin
- foil
- heatproof dish

Ingredients:

- 90 g (3 oz) dried dates, stones removed
- 100 ml (1/5 pt) boiling water
- 1/2 teaspoon bicarbonate of soda
- 45 g (1 1/2 oz) unsalted butter
- 75 g (2 1/2 oz) caster sugar
- 1 medium egg
- 45 g (1 1/2 oz) plain flour
- 45 g (1 1/2 oz) self-raising flour

For the toffee sauce:

- 105 g (3 1/2 oz) demerara sugar
- 60 g (2 oz) butter
- 75 ml (2 1/2 fl.oz) double cream
- vanilla essence

1 Preheat the oven to 180°C / 350°F / gas mark 4. Grease the pudding basin well with butter.

2 Ask an adult to soak the dates in boiling water, then allow to cool. Add the bicarbonate of soda and mix together.

3 Cream the butter and sugar together and beat in the egg. Carefully fold in both flours and mix in the cooled date mixture to form a sloppy dough.

4 Pour the mixture into the buttered pudding basin and cover the top with foil. Seal the edges and place in the oven for approximately 30–40 minutes, or until firm to the touch.

5 To make the toffee sauce, mix all the ingredients together in a small saucepan and heat until simmering. Cook until the sauce has turned a medium shade of brown.

6 To serve, tip the pudding into a deep-sided, heatproof dish and pour over the hot toffee sauce.

7 Place the dish under a hot grill for a few seconds to allow the toffee sauce to bubble. Serve immediately.

TOP TIP! Serve with double cream or vanilla ice cream.

CRACKLE CAKE SLICES

Extra equipment:
- 20 cm (8 in) square baking tin

Ingredients:
- 5 caramel chocolate bars, chopped
- 150 g (5 oz) butter, chopped, plus extra for greasing
- 100 g (3 ½ oz) puffed rice cereal

To decorate:
- 75 g (3 oz) white chocolate

1 Grease the baking tin well with butter.

2 Place a heatproof bowl over a pan of simmering water, making sure the base doesn't touch the water.

3 Place the caramel chocolate bars and butter into the bowl, stirring until melted and well combined. The mixture will curdle but keep stirring until it becomes smooth.

4 Take the bowl off the pan and mix in the puffed rice cereal until well combined with the chocolate mixture.

5 Spoon the mixture into the tin, pressing into the corners and sides and smoothing the top. Allow to cool.

6 Place another heatproof bowl over the pan of simmering water, making sure the base doesn't touch the water. Place the white chocolate in the bowl and stir until melted.

7 Drizzle the melted white chocolate over the cooled chocolate crackle cake and leave to cool and set.

8 Place the chocolate crackle cake in the fridge until set, preferably overnight. Cut into slices while still in the tin, then remove and serve.

TOP TIP!
Add raisins or glacé cherries to the mixture for a fruity alternative.

PEPPERMINT CREAMS

Extra equipment:
- small round cookie cutter
- baking tray

Ingredients:
- I egg white
- 1/2 lemon, juice only
- I teaspoon peppermint flavouring
- 425 g (15 oz) icing sugar
- green food colouring

1 Whisk the egg white in a bowl until it forms stiff peaks. Slowly whisk in the lemon juice, peppermint flavouring and icing sugar until you have a stiff paste.

2 Divide the mixture in half. Add a few drops of green food colouring to one half of the paste, until it is the desired colour and mix well.

3 Place both mixtures onto a work surface, dust with icing sugar and roll each out to about I cm (1/2 in) thick.

4 Cut out small circles from both mixtures using a cookie cutter and place onto the baking tray.

5 Put the peppermint creams in the refrigerator for 1-2 hours, or until the mixture has set.

TOP TIP!
Try coating your peppermint creams in 150 g (6 oz) melted dark chocolate.

YULETIDE FLAPJACKS

Extra equipment:
- 30 x 25.5 cm (12 x 10 in) baking tray
- baking paper

Ingredients:
- 225 g (8 oz) unsalted butter, plus extra for greasing
- 2 tablespoons golden syrup
- 450 g (1 lb) porridge oats
- 225 g (8 oz) soft light brown sugar
- 1 tablespoon ground ginger
- 1/2 teaspoon baking powder
- pinch ground nutmeg
- 1 piece stem ginger in syrup, finely chopped

1 Preheat the oven to 180°C / 350°F / gas mark 4. Grease and line the baking tray.

2 Put the butter and golden syrup into a saucepan and melt over a gentle heat, stirring continuously, until well mixed.

3 Mix the oats, sugar, ground ginger, baking powder and ground nutmeg in a bowl.

4 Then, pour the butter mixture into the dry ingredients. Mix until well combined, then stir in the chopped stem ginger.

5 Pour the mixture into the baking tray and bake for 25–30 minutes, or until golden brown on top.

6 Remove the flapjacks from the oven and cool in the tin for 10 minutes. Then cut the flapjack into squares and put on a wire rack to cool completely.

TOP TIP!
Melt a little chocolate and drizzle it over the flapjacks for an extra special treat!

54

GINGERBREAD HOUSE

Extra equipment:

- baking paper
- baking tray
- rolling pin
- piping bag
- small bowl

Ingredients:

- 250 g (8 3/4 oz) unsalted butter
- 200 g (7 oz) dark muscovado sugar
- 7 tablespoons golden syrup
- 600 g (1 lb 5 oz) plain flour
- 2 teaspoons bicarbonate of soda
- 4 teaspoons ground ginger

For the icing:

- 2 egg whites
- 500 g (1 lb 2 oz) icing sugar

1 Preheat the oven to 200°C / 400°F / gas mark 6.
Cut out 3 templates from baking paper: roof 14 x 12 cm (5 1/2 x 4 3/4 in), side wall 12 x 9.5 cm (4 3/4 x 3 3/4 in), end wall 17 x 12 cm (6 3/4 x 4 3/4 in). Cut two large corners 7.5 cm x 6 cm (3 x 2 1/3 in) off the end wall for the roof slope.

2 Melt the butter, sugar and syrup in a pan until well combined. Mix the flour, bicarbonate of soda and ginger in a bowl and then stir in the butter mixture to make a stiff dough. If it is too dry, add a little water.

3 Place baking paper onto a work surface and roll out a third of the dough to 6 mm (1/4 in) thick. Use the end wall template to cut out two end wall pieces. Then place onto the baking tray, still on the

baking paper. Repeat with the rest of the dough and the other templates to cut out two side walls and two roof pieces. Bake all pieces for 10–15 minutes, or until firm. Place on a wire rack to cool.

4 Mix the egg whites and icing sugar to form a thick, smooth icing. Pipe icing onto the edges of each wall piece and join together. Place a small bowl to support the walls from the inside, and leave to set for 2–3 hours.

5 When set, remove the bowl. Ice the edges of the walls and roof pieces and place on top, holding in place for a few minutes until the icing starts to set. Leave to set completely for 2–3 hours. Use the rest of the icing to decorate the roof and walls of your gingerbread house.

TOP TIP!
Use sweets to decorate the outside of your house!

CHOCOLATE FUDGE

Extra equipment:

- 15 cm (6 in) square baking tin
- greaseproof paper

Ingredients:

- 300 g (10 oz) dark chocolate
- 200 ml (7 fl.oz) condensed milk
- 2 teaspoons vanilla essence

1 Line the tin with greaseproof paper.

2 Ask an adult to help you put the dark chocolate, condensed milk and vanilla essence into a saucepan over a medium heat. Stir them together until the chocolate has melted.

3 Ask an adult to pour the mixture into the tin, and smooth the top with the back of a spoon. Put the tin into the fridge for 3–4 hours.

4 Remove the fudge from the tin by lifting it with the greaseproof paper. Turn it out onto a board and peel off the paper.

5 Cut the slab of fudge into squares and serve!

TOP TIP!
Add chopped nuts or dried fruit to the melted mixture for a change of flavour.

CHRISTMAS PUNCH

SERVES 6

Ingredients:

- 1 litre (2 1/4 pints) apple juice
- 5 whole cloves
- 1 stick cinnamon, broken into pieces
- 50 ml (1 3/4 fl.oz) blackcurrant cordial
- sugar, to taste

1 Put the apple juice, cloves and roughly broken cinnamon stick into a saucepan. Ask an adult to heat gently, just below boiling, for 5 minutes.

2 Add the blackcurrant cordial and mix well. Add sugar to taste, if required.

3 Pour the liquid into a heatproof jug and place into the refrigerator to cool.

4 Once cool, strain the liquid and discard the spices.

5 Pour into glasses and garnish with a cinnamon stick.

TOP TIP! Have this punch hot for a warming drink before bedtime.

APPLE SPICE MUFFINS

Extra equipment:
- muffin tray
- paper cases

Ingredients:
- 110 g (4 oz) butter
- 135 g (5 oz) sugar
- 2 eggs
- 1/2 teaspoon ground cinnamon
- 1/2 teaspoon ground allspice
- 2 teaspoons baking powder
- 1/2 teaspoon bicarbonate of soda
- 235 ml (8 fl.oz) apple sauce
- 190 g (7 oz) plain flour

For the topping:
- 2 tablespoons water
- 120 g (4 oz) icing sugar
- nuts of your choice

1 Preheat the oven to 180°C / 350°F / gas mark 4.

2 In a large bowl mix together the butter and sugar until the mixture is creamy.

3 Add in the eggs and beat until smooth. Blend in the cinnamon, allspice, baking powder and bicarbonate of soda.

4 Add the apple sauce and sift in the flour. Stir until just blended together.

5 Use a teaspoon to divide the mixture equally into the paper cases in the muffin tray. Place the muffins in the oven and bake for 20 minutes, or until a skewer inserted comes out clean. Leave to cool on a wire rack.

6 Mix the icing sugar and water together until they form a smooth paste. Spoon a little icing over each muffin.

7 Top with a few nuts to decorate.

TOP TIP!
Eat these muffins with a hot drink for a real winter treat!

SUGARED PARTY MIX

Extra equipment:
- baking tray
- greaseproof paper

Ingredients:
- 200 g (7 oz) mixed nuts and plain pretzels
- 110 g (4 oz) caster sugar
- 2 tablespoons butter
- 1/2 teaspoon vanilla extract
- 3/4 teaspoon salt

1 Ask an adult to put the mixed nuts and pretzels, sugar and butter in a saucepan over a medium heat.

2 Stir constantly until the nuts are toasted and the sugar has melted and become golden brown, after about 15 minutes.

3 Stir in the vanilla extract.

4 Carefully pour onto a baking tray covered in greaseproof paper and sprinkle with the salt.

5 Leave to cool completely and then break the mixture apart.

TOP TIP!
Serve individual portions in paper cases for a great party snack!

CHRISTMAS ROULADE

Extra equipment:
- 25 x 35 cm (10 x 15 in) Swiss roll tin
- greaseproof paper
- tea towel

Ingredients:
- 5 eggs
- 125 g (4 1/2 oz) caster sugar
- 50 g (1 3/4 oz) butter, melted, plus extra for greasing
- 145 g (5 oz) plain flour
- 50 g (1 3/4 oz) hazelnuts, chopped

For the filling:
- 200 ml (7 fl.oz) double cream

To decorate:
- mixed berries

1. Preheat the oven to 200°C / 400°F / gas mark 6. Grease and line the Swiss roll tin with the greaseproof paper.

2. Crack the eggs into a large bowl. Add the sugar and whisk until the mixture is pale and thickened. Stir in the melted butter and then sift in the flour. Mix together.

3. Pour the mixture into the Swiss roll tin and level the top with the back of a spoon. Place in the oven and bake for 10–12 minutes, or until risen and cooked through.

4. Place a clean tea towel onto a work surface and turn out the cake onto it. Leave the cake to cool for five minutes and then remove the greaseproof paper.

5. Scatter the chopped hazelnuts on top of the cake.

6. For the filling, whip the cream until it forms soft peaks. Spread about three-quarters of the cream evenly over the cake. Carefully, roll up the roulade and place it on a serving dish.

7. Spread the remaining cream over the top of the roulade and decorate with mixed berries.

TOP TIP! Milk and white chocolate buttons make a great alternative topping.

STICKY POPCORN

Ingredients:
- 2 tablespoons sunflower oil
- 100 g (4 oz) popping corn
- 25 g (1 oz) butter

For the toffee:
- 50 g (2 oz) butter
- 50 g (2 oz) brown sugar
- 2 tablespoons golden syrup
- pinch of salt

1 Heat the oil in a large saucepan and sprinkle in the popcorn, making sure that it is coated evenly in oil.

2 Next, cover with a lid, turn the heat down, and listen for popping noises. As soon as the popping quietens down, take the pan off the heat.

3 Next, make the toffee sauce – melt the butter, add the brown sugar and golden syrup in a pan and stir over a high heat for 1–2 minutes.

4 For plain popcorn, tip half of the popcorn out of the saucepan and into a bowl. Toss with 25 g (1 oz) of butter and a pinch of salt.

5 For toffee popcorn, pour the toffee sauce over the remaining popcorn, replace the lid on the pan and shake to mix together well.

6 Pour out into a bowl and serve!

TOP TIP! Make a little extra and string up some popcorn on your Christmas tree!

CHRISTMAS CHOCOLATES

Extra equipment:
- shaped chocolate moulds
- cooking thermometer
- tea towel

Ingredients:
- 100 g (3 ½ oz) good quality milk chocolate
- a little sunflower oil, for the moulds

1 Dampen a piece of kitchen towel with a little sunflower oil and grease each mould. This will create a polished finish on the chocolates and help to release them once set.

2 Place a heatproof bowl over a pan of simmering water, making sure the bowl doesn't touch the water. Break the chocolate into small pieces and place it in the bowl.

3 Ask an adult to place the cooking thermometer in the chocolate and heat until it reaches 43°C / 110°F. Then, remove from the heat and cool to 35°C / 95°F.

4 Pour the melted chocolate into each of the moulds. Use a spatula to scrape off any excess chocolate from the base and then gently tap the moulds on the work surface to remove any air bubbles. Leave the chocolates to set.

5 Once set, turn over the mould onto a clean tea towel and gently remove. Be careful not to handle the chocolates too much or they will begin to melt.

TOP TIP! Repeat this process with plain and white chocolate and give them as gifts to friends and family!

ROCKY ROAD

Extra equipment:
- 24 cm (9 in) baking tin
- clean freezer bag
- rolling pin
- spatula

Ingredients:
- 125 g (4 1/2 oz) butter, softened
- 300 g (10 1/2 oz) dark chocolate, broken into pieces
- 45 ml (1 1/2 fl.oz) golden syrup
- 200 g (7 oz) digestive biscuits
- 100 g (3 1/2 oz) mini marshmallows
- 2 teaspoons icing sugar, for dusting

1 Grease the baking tin with a little butter. Ask an adult to melt the butter, chocolate and golden syrup in a saucepan. When melted, mix well and then spoon out about 125 ml (4 fl.oz) and put to one side.

2 Put the biscuits into a freezer bag and break up with a rolling pin until you have a mixture of fine crumbs and small pieces.

3 Mix the biscuit pieces into the melted chocolate mixture in the saucepan, and then add the marshmallows.

4 Tip into the baking tin and flatten with a spatula. Pour the reserved melted chocolate mixture on top and smooth again.

5 Refrigerate for about 2 hours, or preferably overnight.

6 To serve, cut into 24 fingers and dust with icing sugar.

TOP TIP!
A slice of rocky road wrapped in brightly coloured foil makes a great gift for friends!

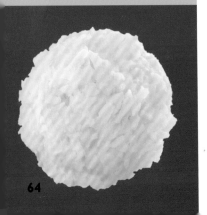

INDEX OF RECIPES

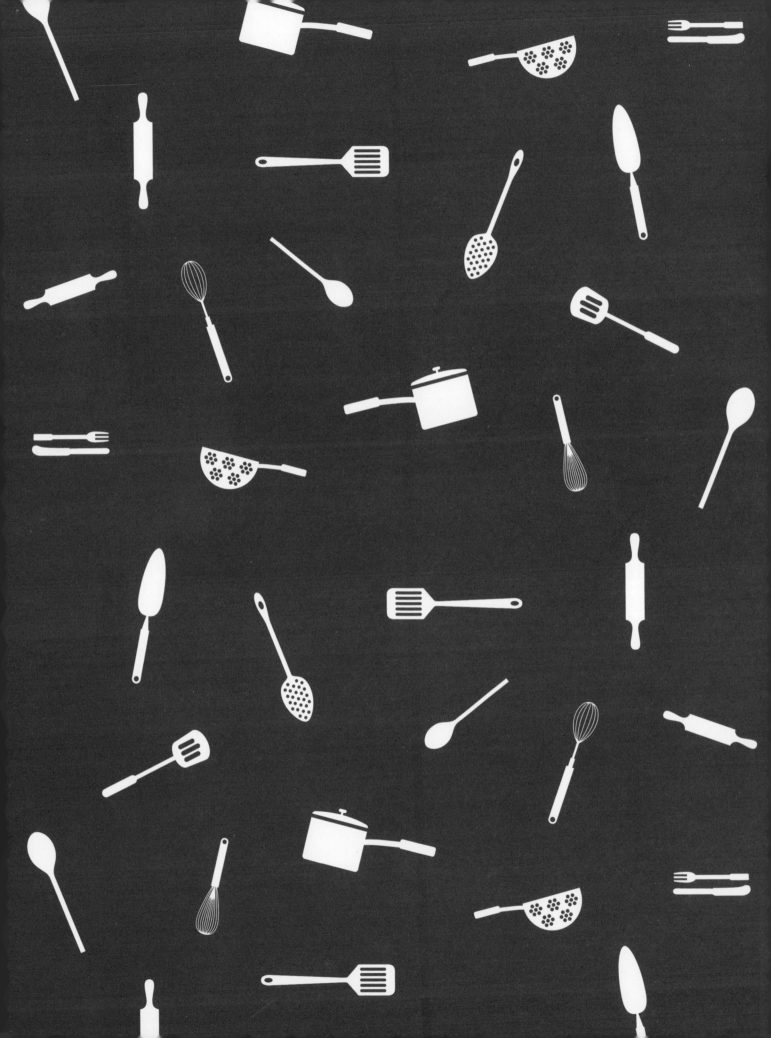